30 DAYS

OF SCRIPTURE INSPIRATION

JAMES L. MILLARD

TREE OF LIFE

FROM

WITH

LOVE

TREE OF LIFE

The Bible is the world's number one bestseller, giving people around the world wisdom, inspiration and encouragement for more than 4,000 years! "Tree of Life" is designed to introduce you to some of the timeless treasures found in the Bible.

Our desire is that you get a taste of the fruit from the "Tree of Life" through reading the passages in this short book, which includes an assortment of well-known Bible verses on a variety of topics that speak to common human needs, problems and issues.

Thirty topics are covered in this book, one for each of the 30 days. Each day includes 3 to 5 verses from different parts of the Bible. Please consider reading one page a day for a month.

We have paraphrased the verses in this book after comparing multiple popular translations of the Bible. An attempt was made to put each verse into natural language that is easy to understand and that captures the intended meaning of each passage.

Please discuss the verses you read with your friends, especially with the person who gave you this book. The following questions may aid your discussion:

> Which verses interested you?
> Which verses inspired you?
> Which verses touched your heart?
> Which verses brought questions to your mind?

With Gratitude
We are especially grateful to John Iwasaki of Bellevue, Washington, for patiently editing this document as well as offering many helpful comments.

DEFINITIONS AND NOTES

Below are basic definitions of a few key words used in the Bible that readers may not be familiar with, and notes to add clarity to this document.

Kingdom of God: This refers to the presence and rule of Christ. The Kingdom of God is both present and future.

Lord: This usually refers to God or to Jesus. It also is used in some cases to mean ruler or master.

LORD: In the Old Testament, LORD (capitalized) is used to refer to the personal name of God (Jehovah), which emphasizes that He is the true and living God who is present everywhere.

Quotations from Jesus Christ: These will be within quotation marks and italicized, as in the following example: *"I am the way, the truth and the life."*

Quotations from the LORD: These will be within quotation marks but not italicized.

Sunrise International Ministries
www.sunriseinternational.org

30 DAYS OF INSPIRATION

H E A R T

- - - - - - - - - - - -

"People look at the outward appearance,
but God looks at the heart."
1 Samuel 16:7

- - - - - - - - -

Above all else, guard your heart!
The real issues of life flow from the heart.
Proverbs 4:23

- - - - - - - - -

"How blessed are people who have a pure heart!
They will see God."
Matthew 5:8

- - - - - - - - -

"Wherever your treasure is, your heart is also there!"
Matthew 6:21

- - - - - - - - -

"What people say comes out of the overflow
of their hearts."
Luke 6:45

DAY

1

heart

W O R R Y

- - - - - - - - - - - - -

*"Do not worry about your life. Don't worry about what you
will eat or drink. Don't worry about what you will wear. Isn't
life much more than food or clothes? Look at the birds of the
air. They do not plant seeds or store food in barns, but your
Father in heaven feeds them very well. You are much more
valuable than the birds! And, you cannot even add a single
hour to your life by worrying!"*
Matthew 6:25-27

- - - - - - - - -

*"Seek first the Kingdom of God (the rule and presence of
Christ) and the righteous life that He desires for us. Then
everything else you need will be given to you as well. Don't
worry about tomorrow! Tomorrow will worry about itself.
Each day has enough trouble of its own."*
Matthew 6:33-34

- - - - - - - - -

*"Do not let your heart be troubled.
Trust in God and trust also in me."*
John 14:1

- - - - - - - - -

Give all of your worries to God because
He loves you and cares for you!
I Peter 5:7

DAY

2 worry.

P E A C E

- - - - - - - - - - -

"Peace I leave with you. I give you my peace! I do not give you peace like the world gives. Do not let your heart be troubled and do not be afraid."
John 14:27

- - - - - - - - -

May the Lord of peace continually give you
His peace in every situation.
II Thessalonians 3:16

- - - - - - - - -

May the LORD bless you and keep you. May the LORD
make His face shine on you, and may He pour out His
love and mercy to you. May the LORD continue to watch
over you and give you peace.
Numbers 6:24-26

- - - - - - - - -

Don't worry about anything, but in everything talk
with God directly through prayer, with thanksgiving,
and tell God what you need. Then the peace of God,
which surpasses all human understanding will keep your
hearts and minds in Christ Jesus.
Philippians 4:6-7

DAY 3 PEACE

COURAGE

- - - - - - - - - - - - - - - -

"Be strong and courageous. Don't be afraid or
discouraged, because the Lord your God will be with
you wherever you go."
Joshua 1:9

- - - - - - - - -

"Do not fear, for I am with you. Don't be distracted or
discouraged, for I am your God. I will strengthen you,
I will help you and I will uphold you with my righteous
right hand."
Isaiah 41:10

- - - - - - - - -

Wicked people run away even though no one is chasing
them, but righteous people can be as bold as a lion.
Proverbs 28:1

- - - - - - - - -

"Don't be afraid. Just believe."
Mark 5:36

DAY 4

Courage

R E S T

- - - - - - - - -

*"Come to me everyone who is carrying a heavy load. Come all
who are tired and exhausted physically, mentally and
emotionally. Take my yoke and stay connected to me and walk
with me. Learn from me. I am gentle and humble in heart. Then
you will find true rest for your souls. Walking in relationship
with me is easy and the load I give you is light."*
Matthew 11:28-30

- - - - - - - - -

We don't have a high priest who is so far above us that
he cannot understand and sympathize with our weaknesses. Our high priest (Jesus), who represents us
before God, was tempted in every way we are tempted.
However, He did not sin.

So, let us come to the throne of God's grace with
complete confidence, knowing that He understands
our weaknesses and temptations. Then we will receive
mercy and find grace to help us in our time of need.
Hebrews 4:15-16

- - - - - - - - -

My soul finds rest in God alone. My hope comes from
Him. He alone is my rock and my salvation. Because He
is my fortress, I will not be shaken.
Psalm 62:5-6

REST

5

DAY

J O Y

Be joyful always, pray continually and give thanks
in all circumstances.
I Thessalonians 5:16-18

- - - - - - - - -

*"I have said these things to you so that my joy may remain
in you and that your joy may be complete."*
John 15:11

- - - - - - - - -

Consider it pure joy when you face all kinds of trials
and problems because you know that when your faith is
tested it develops perseverance in you.
James 1:2-3

- - - - - - - - -

Those who sow seed with tears will reap with joy. They
who go out weeping to sow seed will return with songs
of great joy, bringing sheaves of the harvest with them.
Psalm 126:5-6

Day 6

JOY

PRAYER & PROMISES

- -

"Ask and you shall receive, seek and you will find,
knock and the door will be opened."
Matthew 7:7-8

- - - - - - - - -

"Whatever you ask God for when you pray, believe that you
have received it and it will be yours."
Mark 11:24

- - - - - - - - - -

This is the confidence we have when we pray to God.
If we ask for anything according to His will, we know
that He hears us. Since we know that He hears us, we
know that we have what we have asked Him for.
I John 5:14-15

- - - - - - - - - -

Those who wait on the Lord will renew their strength.
They will soar on wings like eagles. They will run and
not be weary, they will walk and not faint.
Isaiah 40:31

DAY

7

prayer and promises

W I S D O M

- - - - - - - - - - - - - -

The Lord gives wisdom, and from His mouth come
knowledge and understanding.
Proverbs 2:6

- - - - - - - - -

A person who finds wisdom and gains understanding is
very blessed. Wisdom is more valuable than silver and
more profitable than gold.
Proverbs 3:13-14

- - - - - - - - -

Humbly honoring the Lord is the beginning of wisdom,
and knowing the Holy One is understanding.
Proverbs 9:10

- - - - - - - - -

If any of you lack wisdom, ask God for it and He will
give you wisdom! He gives to everyone generously
without condemning you for all of your faults.
James 1:5

DAY

8

Wisdom

MORE WISDOM

- - - - - - - - - - - - - - - - - -

Pride brings disgrace, but wisdom
comes with humility.
Proverbs 11:2

- - - - - - - - -

It is much better to get wisdom than gold, and to
choose understanding than silver.
Proverbs 16:16

- - - - - - - - -

Wisdom will give you patience. You will be honored
when you overlook insults and offenses.
Proverbs 19:11

- - - - - - - - -

True wisdom that comes from God is first pure,
peaceful, considerate, not self-centered, full of mercy
and good fruit, impartial and sincere.
James 3:17

DAY

more Wisdom

P R I D E

- - - - - - - - - -

Pride goes before destruction, and an arrogant
attitude before a fall.
Proverbs 16:18

- - - - - - - - -

Pride will bring a person down low, but if you
have a humble spirit you will gain honor.
Proverbs 29:23

- - - - - - - - -

God opposes people who are proud, but gives
grace to those who are humble.
I Peter 5:5

- - - - - - - - -

*"Everyone who exalts himself will be
humbled, but everyone who humbles
himself will be exalted."*
Luke 18:14

DAY

10

PRIDE

HUMILITY

----

*"This truth is absolute. If you don't change your attitude
and your heart and become like a little child, you will never
enter the Kingdom of God."*
Matthew 18:3

- - - - - - - - -

Pride brings disgrace and shame, but wisdom
comes with humility.
Proverbs 11:2

- - - - - - - - -

*"People who are humble and admit their needs will be
blessed. The Kingdom of God is theirs."*
Matthew 5:3

- - - - - - - - -

Humble yourselves before God, and he will lift you up.
James 4:10

- - - - - - - - -

*"If you do not receive the Kingdom of God like a little child
you will never enter it."*
Mark 10:15

DAY

11

Humility

W O R D S

- - - - - - - - - - - - - -

Reckless words pierce like a sword, but the words of
the wise bring healing.
Proverbs 12:18

- - - - - - - - -

Life and death are in the tongue. If you love to talk
remember this: You will eat the fruit of what you say.
Proverbs 18:21

- - - - - - - - -

A person who guards his mouth and his tongue keeps
himself out of trouble.
Proverbs 21:23

- - - - - - - - -

The tongue is a small part of the body, but it makes great
boasts. A huge forest fire can be started by a small spark. In
the same way, the tongue is like fire. The tongue is small, but
it can cause great harm. You can pollute your whole being by
what you say. Your tongue starts many fires in your life and
is itself set on fire by forces of evil (hell).
James 3:5-6

- - - - - - - - -

Do not let negative and harmful words come out of your
mouth. Understand the needs of others and say only what is
helpful for building them up. Speak words of grace to them.
Ephesians 4:19

DAY

12 WORDS

H O P E

- - - - - - - - - -

May the God who gives hope fill you with great joy and peace as you trust in Him. Then you will overflow with hope through the power of the Holy Spirit.

Romans 15:13

- - - - - - - - - -

We know that God works everything out for good in the lives of people who love Him and who are called according to His purpose.

Romans 8:28

- - - - - - - - - -

Don't put your hope in the strength of horses. They cannot save you no matter how strong they are. The eyes of the Lord are on people who fear and honor Him, on those who hope in His infinite and amazing love.

Psalm 33:17-18

- - - - - - - - - -

The Lord says, "I know what I am planning for you. I have plans to bless you, not to harm you. They are plans to give you a future filled with hope."

Jeremiah 29:11

G I V I N G

----

*"Give and it will be given to you. Then a large amount,
pressed down, shaken together and running over will be
poured into your lap. The standard you use when you give
to others will be applied to you."*
Luke 6:38

- - - - - - - - -

If you sow only a small amount of seed you will reap
only a small harvest. If you sow generously you will
also reap generously. Let each of us give what we
have decided in our hearts. Do not give reluctantly or
because you feel pressured to give. God loves a person
who gives cheerfully.
II Corinthians 9:6-7

- - - - - - - - -

"It is more blessed to give than to receive."
Acts 20:35

- - - - - - - - -

God loved the world so much that He gave His only Son,
so that whoever believes in Him would not perish, but
have eternal life.
John 3:16

DAY

14

Giving

F A I T H

- - - - - - - - - -

Trust in the Lord with all of your heart. Don't rely on
your own understanding and reasoning. In all of your
ways honor and acknowledge the Lord. He will guide
you in the right way.
Proverbs 3:5-6

- - - - - - - - -

"Everything is possible for the person who believes."
Mark 9:23

- - - - - - - - -

A person who trusts in the Lord and depends on Him
will be abundantly blessed. He will be like a tree
planted by a river that puts its roots into the stream.
The tree has no fear when the heat comes. Its leaves
are always green. Even in the year of drought it has no
worries and never fails to bear fruit.
Jeremiah 17:7-8

- - - - - - - - -

"Nothing is impossible with God."
Luke 1:37

- - - - - - - - -

"According to your faith it will be done for you."
Matthew 9:29

DAY 15

FAITH

FORGIVENESS

- - - - - - - - - - - - - - - - - - - -

Be kind, gentle and loving to one another, forgiving
each other just as God forgave you through Christ.
Ephesians 4:32

- - - - - - - - -

*"Do not judge others or you also will be judged.
You will be judged in the same way that you judge
others. The same standard you use to
judge others will be used for you."*
Matthew 7:1-2

- - - - - - - - -

*When you pray, and you know in your heart that
you are angry or are judging someone, forgive them before
God. Then you can receive forgiveness
for your sins from your Father."*
Mark 11:25

- - - - - - - - -

Be patient with one another and forgive each
other no matter what problems or complaints
you have against someone else. Freely forgive
others just as the Lord freely forgave you.
Colossians 3:13

DAY

16

forgiveness

H A R M O N Y

- - - - - - - - - - - - - - - -

Above all, love each other. Love binds everything
together in perfect harmony.
Colossians 3:14

- - - - - - - - -

Don't do anything for selfish reasons or for empty
pride. Humble yourself and honor others above
yourself. Don't focus on yourself, but focus on others.
Philippians 2:3-4

- - - - - - - - -

*"Do to others what you want them to do to you. This sums
up all the laws and teachings in the Bible."*
Matthew 7:12

- - - - - - - - -

Live in harmony with each other. Don't let pride destroy
your relationships with others. Make friends and spend
time with everyone, even if they are of a lower position
than you. Don't think that you are better than others.
Romans 12:16

DAY

17

harmony

F A M I L Y

- - - - - - - - - - - - -

"Honor your father and your mother so that you may
live long in the land the LORD your God is giving you."
Exodus 20:12

- - - - - - - - -

Children, obey your parents. This is God's will. It is
the right thing to do. And it is the first of the Ten
Commandments given with a promise: "Honor your
father and mother. Then you will be happy and enjoy a
long life on this earth."
Ephesians 6:1-3

- - - - - - - - -

Husband, you must love your wife as you love yourself.
Wife, you must respect your husband.
Ephesians 5:32

- - - - - - - - -

Children are your legacy, a gift from the Lord.
They are a reward from Him.
Psalm 127:3

- - - - - - - - -

Listen to your father, since you are his son. Respect and
honor your mother when she is old.
Proverbs 23:22

DAY

FAMILY

L O V E

- - - - - - - - - -

"This is my main command: Love each other
as I have loved you."
John 15:12

- - - - - - - - -

God is love. Whoever lives in love lives in God,
and God lives in him.
I John 4:16

- - - - - - - - -

Above all, love each other deeply from the heart,
because love forgives and forgets mountains of sins.
I Peter 4:8

- - - - - - - - -

Even if I can speak many languages, if I don't have love,
my words are just noise. I may be able to prophesy,
understand deep mysteries and have great knowledge.
I may also have great faith that can move mountains.
But if I do not have genuine love, I am nothing. And
even if I give everything I own to poor people or make
great personal sacrifices, if I do not have love I have
accomplished nothing really important.
I Corinthians 13:1-3

DAY

19

LOVE.

CREATION

- - - - - - - - - - - - - - - -

In the beginning God created the heavens
and the earth.
Genesis 1:1

- - - - - - - - -

God created mankind in His own image. He created
both men and women in His image.
Genesis 1:27

- - - - - - - - -

God looked at everything He had made,
and it was very good.
Genesis 1:31

- - - - - - - - -

You created my inner being and knit me together
in my mother's womb. I will give thanks to
You because Your work is so
wonderful and amazing.
Psalm 139:13-14

DAY

20

CREATION

GOD'S LOVE

- - - - - - - - - - - - - - - - - -

God loved the world so much that He gave His only
Son, so that whoever believes in Him would
not perish, but have eternal life.
John 3:16

- - - - - - - - -

Anyone who does not love does not know God,
because God is love.
I John 4:8

- - - - - - - - -

This is love, not that we loved God, but that He loved
us and sent His Son to be a sacrifice that forgives and
covers all of our sins.
I John 4:10

- - - - - - - - -

God demonstrated His love for us in this: Christ died
for us while we were still living in sin.
Romans 5:8

DAY

God's Love.

FATHER IN HEAVEN

"If your son asks for bread, would you give him a stone? If he asks for a fish, would you give him a snake? Of course not. We are imperfect human beings, but we give good gifts to our children. How much more will your Father in heaven give good gifts to those who ask Him."
Matthew 7:9-11

- - - - - - - - -

As a father has compassion for his children, so the Lord has compassion for those who fear and honor Him. He knows how we were formed, and knows that we are made of dust.
Psalm 103:13-14

- - - - - - - - -

"Anyone who has seen me has seen the Father. Don't you understand that I am in the Father, and that the Father is in me? The words I say to you are not my own. It is the Father living in me who is doing His work."
John 14:9-10

- - - - - - - - -

He got up and decided to return to his father. But while he was still a long way off, his father saw him and was filled with compassion for him; he ran to his son, threw his arms around him and kissed him.
Luke 15:20

DAY

22

Father in Heaven.

FORGIVENESS OF SIN

- -

The Lord is compassionate and merciful, slow to anger,
abounding in love. He will not always accuse us or be
angry with us. He does not treat us according to our
sins or repay us for our wrongs.

As high as the heavens are above the earth, that is how
great His love is towards those who fear and honor
Him. As far as the east is from the west, that is how far
He has removed our sins from us.

Psalm 103:8-12

- - - - - - - - -

If we confess our sins to God He will forgive our sins
and purify us from all unrighteousness, because He is
faithful and just.

I John 1:9

- - - - - - - - -

"I will forgive their wickedness and will not remember
their sins."

Hebrews 8:12

DAY

23

forgiveness of sin

TRUE LIFE

- - - - - - - - - - - - - - - -

*"I have come that they may experience true life and com-
plete fullness of heart."*
John 10:10

- - - - - - - - -

*"Human beings do not live on bread alone, but by every
word that God speaks to us."*
Matthew 4:4

- - - - - - - - -

*"I am the bread of life. Anyone who comes to me will never
be hungry, and whoever believes in me will
never be thirsty."*
John 6:35

- - - - - - - - -

*"If anyone is thirsty, let him come to me and drink. Who-
ever believes in me, as the Scriptures say, living water will
flow from his innermost being."*
John 7:37-39

- - - - - - - - -

*"I am the light of the world. Whoever follows me will not
walk in darkness, but will have the light of life."*
John 8:12

DAY

24

TRU3 LIF3

THE GOOD SHEPHERD

- -

*Jesus said, "I am the good shepherd. The good shepherd
lays down His life for the sheep."*
John 10:11

- - - - - - - - -

The Lord is my Shepherd. He takes care of me and
provides everything I need. I lack nothing.

He makes me lie down in green pastures and leads me
by quiet waters, a place of peace and rest.

He restores my soul when I am hurting and broken. He
guides me in the right path because He is righteous.

Even if I face death and walk through the valley of the
shadow of death, I will fear no evil, for You are with me.
What a comfort to know that You guide and protect me
with Your rod and staff.

You pour out blessings on me even in the presence of
my enemies. You refresh me with the life of Your Spirit.
My cup overflows with blessings from You.

Surely goodness and mercy will follow me all the days of
my life, and I will dwell in the house of the Lord forever.
Psalm 23:1-6

DAY

25

The Good Shepherd

HOLY SPIRIT

- - - - - - - - - - - - - - - - - - - -

"God is spirit. People who worship God must worship Him in spirit and in truth."
John 4:24

- - - - - - - - -

"The wind blows in many directions. You can hear the sound of the wind, but cannot tell where it comes from or where it is going. The same is true everyone who is born of the Spirit. You cannot completely explain or predict the work of God's Spirit through human wisdom and logic."
John 3:8

- - - - - - - - - -

God gave this promise about the last days: "I will pour out my Spirit on all people. Your sons and daughters will prophesy. Your young men will see visions and your old men will dream dreams."
Acts 2:17

- - - - - - - - -

It is written in the Old Testament: "No eye has seen, no ear has heard, and no mind has conceived what God has prepared for those who love Him." But God has revealed it to us by His Spirit.
I Corinthians 2:9-10

DAY

26

Holy Spirit

WORK OF THE SPIRIT

- -

"When the Spirit of truth comes, He will guide
you into all truth."
John 16:13

- - - - - - - - -

We have not received the spirit of this world, but
we have received the Spirit of God, so that we may
understand what He has freely given us.
I Corinthians 2:12

- - - - - - - - -

We know that we live in Him and He in us, because He
has given us of His Spirit.
I John 4:13

- - - - - - - - -

The fruit of the Spirit of God is love, joy, peace,
patience, kindness, goodness, faithfulness,
gentleness and self-control.
Galatians 5:22-23

DAY 27

WORK OF THE SPIRIT

G R A C E

- - - - - - - - - - - - -

For you know the grace of our Lord Jesus
Christ. Though He was rich, yet for your sake
He became poor, so that you through
His poverty might become rich.
II Corinthians 8:9

- - - - - - - - -

"My grace is sufficient for you, for my power
is made perfect in weakness."
II Corinthians 12:9

- - - - - - - - - -

May the grace of the Lord Jesus Christ,
and the love of God, and the fellowship
of the Holy Spirit be with you all.
II Corinthians 13:14

DAY

28

GRACE.

MORE GRACE

- - - - - - - - - - - - - - - - -

Out of the abundance of His grace we have received
blessing upon blessing. The Law was given through
Moses, but grace and truth came through Jesus Christ.
John 1:16-17

- - - - - - - - -

God makes us right before Him through the free gift of
His grace. Jesus paid the price to set us free.
Romans 3:24

- - - - - - - - -

May our Lord Jesus Christ Himself and God our
Father, who loved us and by His grace gave us eternal
encouragement and good hope, encourage your hearts
and strengthen you in every good deed and word.
II Thessalonians 2:16-17

- - - - - - - - -

You have been saved by God's grace through believing
what Christ has done for you. Salvation is a gift from
God, not something you have earned through your
efforts or good works. Therefore no one has
any reason to boast.
Ephesians 2:8-9

DAY

29

more grace

MORE LOVE

- - - - - - - - - - - - - - - - - -

Love each other with deep affection, from the heart
as true brothers. Honor each another above yourself.
Romans 12:10

- - - - - - - - -

Let us not love only with our words and mouth,
but with our actions and in truth.
I John 3:18

- - - - - - - - -

Whoever does not love does not know God,
because God is love.
I John 4:8

- - - - - - - - -

Anyone who does not love his brother, whom he can
see with his eyes, cannot love God, whom he cannot see
with his eyes.
I John 4:20

- - - - - - - - -

*"Love your enemies, do good to people who hate you, bless
those who curse you, and pray for people who treat you
badly."*

Luke 6:27-28

DAY 30 more love.